AUGUSTA THE GREAT

by ANGUS McGILL & DOMINIC POELSMA

BARRIE & JENKINS
COMMUNICA - EUROPA

First published in 1977 by
Barrie and Jenkins Ltd
24 Highbury Crescent London N5 1RX

ISBN 0 214 20481 2

Printed in Great Britain at the Alden Press, Oxford

'LOOK, WHY DON'T YOU TALK TO HER ABOUT IT? SHE'S ALL RIGHT. SHE'LL UNDERSTAND.

NO WASHING WITHOUT ASKING

RIGHT!

MUMMY! CAN I HAVE A WORD WITH YOU? IT'S ABOUT MY FACE! IT'S **MY** FACE, YOU SEE, AND I DON'T THINK YOU SHOULD KEEP...

KEEP WHAT?

NEVER MIND!

FRIENDS... OR ANYWAY, FRIEND...

NO WASHING WITHOUT ASKING!

SAVE OUR FACES!

SAVE OUR FACES RALLY

LET US UNITE AGAINST THE FACE WASHERS. LET US SAVE OUR FACES BEFORE IT IS TOO LATE. UNITED WE STAND...

AUGUSTA!

WHAT A DIRTY FACE!

... DIVIDED WE FALL...

SAVE OUR FACES RALLY

LET'S PLAY MUHAMMAD ALI AND SOCRATES. I'LL BE MUHAMMAD ALI AND YOU BE SOCRATES.

OKAY!

I AM THE GREATEST!

THIS TIME **I'M** MUHAMMAD ALI AND **YOU** BE SOCRATES!

OKAY. **I'M** SOCRATES AND **YOU** ARE MUHAMMAD ALI.

I AM THE GREATEST!

Poelsma

CAN YOU SKIP, GRANDMA?

SKIP? GOOD GRACIOUS CHILD, I CAN'T REMEMBER. LET ME SEE...

SALT, VINEGAR, MUSTARD, PEPPER. SALT, VINEGAR, MUSTARD, PEPPER.

YES I CAN SKIP.

GRANDMA BRAVO! SHOW GRANDMA QUINCY HOW YOU CAN SKIP!

PEASE PUDDING HOT PEASE PUDDING COLD PEASE PUDDING IN THE POT FIVE DAYS OLD...

THANK YOU!

HAIL TO THEE BLITHE SPIRIT, BIRD THOU NEVER WERT...

THERE WAS A SMALL GIRL CALLED AUGUSTA··

THAT'S ME! LISTEN EVERYBODY! THAT'S ME!

WHO RAISED ALL THE STRENGTH SHE COULD MUSTER...

SHH! BE QUIET! LISTEN TO THIS GOOD POEM ABOUT ME!

AND WITHOUT MORE ADO JOINED UP WITH THE SIOUX...

JOINED UP WITH THE SIOUX! TEE HEE HEE!

BET YOU WISH **YOU'D** DONE THAT GENERAL CUSTER!

GENERAL WHO? WAIT A BIT! GENERAL WHO?

MUMMY SAYS YOU HAD A BEAUTIFUL WHITE WEDDING, GRANDMA.

WELL, YES, DARLING, IT WAS **FAIRLY** BEAUTIFUL...

THEN I HAD A WHITE DIVORCE!

THAT WAS **REALLY** BEAUTIFUL!

WHEN I MARRIED YOUR FATHER, DARLING I HAD THE **MOST** DIVINE DRESS.

IT WAS ALL DAZZLING WHITE CHIFFON WITH A GREAT BILLOWING VEIL AND A TRAIN 10 YARDS LONG.

OR WAS IT A LITTLE BLUE CHANEL SUIT,..? OR A GOLD LAMÉ SHEATH,? OR A SIMPLE BLACK BALENCIAGA WITH PEARLS...

REALLY MOTHER! SURELY YOU REMEMBER YOUR WEDDING DRESS!

YES OF COURSE DARLING. I REMEMBER THE DRESSES IN EVERY DETAIL...

IT'S THE HUSBANDS I CAN'T RECALL...

CAN YOU PUT YOUR OWN SHOES ON YET?

OF COURSE I CAN!

JUST AS LONG AS MUM GIVES A SORT OF PULL AND A PUSH AND A KIND OF TWIST AND A SORT OF RUNNY ROUND WITH HER FINGER...

TEE HEE HEE
HEE HEE HEE
HEE

SPOIL SPORT!

TEE
HEE HEE
TEE HEE HEE

YOU'VE SQUASHED
OUR LOVELY BANANA SKIN!

TEE HEE HEE
HEE HEE

EXCUSE ME
IS THIS **YOUR**
BANANA SKIN?

NO!

NO IT ISN'T
IT ISN'T **OURS**

CERTAINLY **NOT!**

OH GOOD I'VE BEEN
LOOKING FOR A
LOVELY BANANA SKIN!

HO HO HO
HO HO

CLIVE. WHO AM I MEANT TO BE?

I KNOW. YOU'RE ... OH, YOU KNOW, WHO'S THE ONE WHO LOOKS LIKE THAT AGAIN?

ROBIN DAY?

THAT'S HIM! ROBIN DAY!

WRONG!

THIS IS MRS FOSDICK, DARLING. THE ONE WHO READS TEA-CUPS.

OH GOODIE! WOULD YOU READ MY LEMONADE GLASS FIRST?

BEWARE THE IDES OF MARCH!

NEXT!

SHH. MRS FOSDICK IS READING MY TEA-CUP!

WHAT DOES IT SAY?

IT SAYS THERE WILL BE A LETTER AND A VISIT FROM A STRANGER AND BEWARE THE IDES OF MARCH AND A JOURNEY AND GOOD NEWS FROM AFAR...

Poelsma

THE USUAL!

POOR FIEND FROM OUTER SPACE!

YOU'VE JUST MISSED THE FIEND FROM OUTER SPACE!

THE FIEND WAS LIKE A HUGE YELLOW SPIDER THING AND IT WOVE WEBS OVER WHOLE CITIES AND ATE PEOPLE...

THEN THEY BOMBED HIM!

POOR FIEND FROM OUTER SPACE!

MUMMY, WHEN I GROW UP, CAN I BE A FIEND FROM OUTER SPACE?

NO DEAR.

I KNEW I COULDN'T REALLY...

WHEN I GROW UP I'M GOING TO BE...

KOJAK...

MUMMY! ITS THE BURGLAR!

I'M NOT A BURGLAR! I'M A NICE LADY IN A FUR COAT AS ALL CAN SEE...

HOW DO YOU DO!

NICE LADIES IN FUR COATS GET ASKED IN FOR TEA.

OH. YES. WELL, WOULD YOU LIKE A CUP OF TEA?

JUST LEAVE YOUR BAG IN THE HALL!

SWAG

TELL ME. HOW ARE YOU BURGLARS DOING THESE DAYS?

I AM NOT A BURGLAR! I AM A NICE LADY IN A FUR COAT WHO HAS CALLED FOR TEA.

MILK? SUGAR?

BUT I CAN TELL YOU THIS. WE NICE LADIES IN FUR COATS ARE DOING VERY BADLY!

TEA SPOONS HARDLY PAY THE RENT.

WELL... MUST BE DASHING ALONG...

AH. YES. WELL EXCUSE ME BUT I RATHER THINK YOU PUT MY TEA SPOON IN ERROR INTO YOUR HANDBAG!

ME? GOOD HEAVENS! WHAT ARE YOU SUGGESTING? THERE'S NOTHING IN MY HANDBAG...

EXCEPT A LITTLE SPARE CUTLERY.

IT COULD HAPPEN TO ANYONE!

CHARMED I'M SURE!

HELLO, GRANDMA! GUESS WHAT I'M DIGGING!

WELL NOW. HOW MANY GUESSES DO I HAVE? LET ME THINK. ER... UM... A HOLE?

SOMEONE TOLD YOU!

CERTAINLY NOT!

THOUGH DEAR CLIVE DID DROP A TEENSIE HINT!

HEY CLIVE!

WHAT?

IF I GO DOWN AND DOWN TILL I COME OUT THE OTHER SIDE, WHERE WOULD I BE?

WELL— AUSTRALIA I SUPPOSE.

AUSTRALIA?

FORGET IT!

OH AUGUSTA I HEAR YOU'VE BEEN DIGGING IN THE GARDEN!

THAT'S RIGHT GRANDMA.

WELL YOU DIDN'T COME ACROSS THE MIDDLE BUTTON OF THIS CARDIGAN, DID YOU?

NO. WHEN DID YOU LOSE IT?

1936.

HELLO! HELL-O! HEL-LO! **HELLO!**

COME ON! SAY IT! HELLO···HELLO··· HELLO··· HELLO···

HELLO!

HE'S SHY!

WHAT'S AUGUSTA UP TO?

SHE'S COACHING CRIPPEN FOR RICHARD III!

BUT THAT'S RIDICULOUS!

NOW IS THE WINTER OF OUR DISCONTENT···

··MADE GLORIOUS SUMMER BY THIS SUN OF YORK···

THE CAT IS COMPLETELY MISCAST···

HELLO!

HELLO? IS THAT ALL YOU CAN SAY?

'HELLO' IS MORE THAN YOUR STUPID DOG CAN SAY!

OUR STUPID DOG SAYS A LOT!

WHAT FOR INSTANCE?

BOW WOW FOR INSTANCE!

BOW WOW! SAY BOW WOW!

HELLO!

HE ALSO KNOWS QUITE A LOT OF KIPLING, DON'T YOU SOLOMON?

BOW WOW!

 HELLO LITTLE GIRL... ARE YOU LOST?
 LOST? OH. WELL, YES I SUPPOSE I MUST BE.
 WHAAAAAAAA!

 THIS POOR LITTLE GIRL HAS LOST HER MOMMY...
 OH DEAR! WELL NOW! WHAT DOES YOUR MOMMY LOOK LIKE?
 SHE'S A HUGE, PINK LADY WITH GREAT BIG HANDS AND GREAT LONG ARMS AND AN ENORMOUS RED MOUTH AND HUGE BIG TEETH.
 YOU'RE QUITE SURE YOU WANT TO FIND HER?

 ALL RIGHT. NOW WE HAVE YOUR DESCRIPTION OF YOUR MOMMY. WE'LL SOON FIND HER FOR YOU.
 ATTENTION, PLEASE...
 IF A HUGE, PINK LADY CALLED MRS. BRAVO IS IN THE STORE, WOULD SHE COME TO INFORMATION WHERE HER LITTLE GIRL IS WAITING!
 JUST WAIT TILL I GET YOU HOME... BUT YOU **ARE** A HUGE, PINK LADY!

MUMMY IT'S THE BURGLAR!

I AM NOT A BURGLAR. I AM A KINDLY PERSON WHO, DEVOTED TO GOOD WORKS, IS SPENDING HIS LEISURE HOURS COLLECTING FOR A JUMBLE SALE, AS ALL CAN SEE!

BUT HOW NICE! WHAT IS YOUR STALL GOING TO BE?

CASH, FURS AND COSTLY JEWELS!

DARLING... LOOK WHO'S HERE! IT'S THE BURGLAR!

HOW D'YOU DO.

I AM NOT A BURGLAR! I AM A PERSON WHO, DEVOTED TO GOOD WORKS, IS SPENDING HIS LEISURE HOURS COLLECTING FOR A JUMBLE SALE!

A JUMBLE SALE?

I'M COLLECTING CASH, FURS...

...AND COSTLY JEWELS!

YOU HAVE JUST BEEN ELECTED VICE PRESIDENT OF THE GOOD GUYS CLUB!

REALLY?

JUST SWEAR YOU'RE IN FAVOUR OF MOTHERHOOD, DECENCY, WORLD PEACE, AND FREEDOM FOR ALL!

I SWEAR!

GOOD! THAT'S 50 P PLEASE!

YOU DIDN'T MENTION THE 50 P!

YOU HAVE JUST BEEN ELECTED VICE PRESIDENT OF THE GOOD GUYS CLUB...

GRANDMA... WHAT WAS IT LIKE IN THE OLDEN DAYS?

WELL, DARLING, LITTLE GIRLS WERE KEPT LOCKED UP IN SORT OF PRISONS, CALLED NURSERIES, WITH CRUEL GOVERNESSES ALL DAY LONG AND THEY HAD HORRID TASKS TO PERFORM AND WERE FED ON GRUEL AND WERE SOMETIMES SEEN BUT **NEVER** HEARD...

IT WAS ABSOLUTELY DIVINE!

GRANDMA!

DARLING **MUST** YOU CALL ME THAT?

DO YOU REMEMBER THE WILLIAMS?

THE WILLIAMS? DARLING, IT'S THE WILLIAM**SES**! JOHN AND GLORIA WILLIAMS. MARCIA WILLIAMS. ESTHER WILLIAMS...

NO I MEAN THE WILLIAMS. WILLIAM I, WILLIAM II, WILLIAM III...

MY FAVOURITE IS JUST WILLIAM.

KINDLY ADDRESS ALL FURTHER COMMUNICATIONS TO MY LAWYER...

GRANDMA!

HERE WE GO AGAIN!

DO YOU REMEMBER...

OIL LAMPS? BELISHA BEACONS? NELLIE WALLACE? NO I DO **NOT**!

NO, DO YOU REMEMBER...

MARIE TEMPEST? CLOTHING COUPONS? HEREWARD THE WAKE? CERTAINLY **NOT**!

"WHERE I PUT MY NODDY BOOK?

CRINOLINES? THE FOXTROT? HAROLD WILSON? **LONG** BEFORE MY TIME...

CLIVE, WHAT DO GHOSTS **DO**?

WELL, THEY **HAUNT**, DON'T THEY?

HAUNT? IS THAT **ALL**?

WELL, YES. I THINK SO!

MONEY FOR OLD ROPE!

HAVE **YOU** EVER SEEN A GHOST, GRANDMA?

YES DARLING INDEED I HAVE!

WHAT WAS IT LIKE?

ABSOLUTELY **DIVINE**, DARLING. IT HAD THE SWEETEST LITTLE MOUSTACHE AND SUCH EYES! I RATHER THINK IT WAS FRENCH.

IT CERTAINLY **BEHAVED** FRENCH!

MUMMY. IS THERE A GHOST IN THE HOUSE?

OH NO DEAR. AT LEAST I DON'T THINK SO.

WELL, I DON'T KNOW...

SOMEONE'S FINISHED OFF THE CHOCOLATE ICE CREAM IN THE FRIDGE...

AH! MR & MRS PARKER FROM Nº 3!

CORRECT! WE ARE CONDUCTING A SURVEY INTO THE SEX LIVES OF OUR NEIGHBOURS. WHAT WE WANT TO KNOW IS WHAT YOU GET UP TO.

OH. I SEE. WHO DID YOU SAY YOU WERE DOING THIS FOR?

MRS BRAVO! WHAT ARE YOU SUGGESTING? WE AREN'T DOING IT FOR ANYONE...

WE JUST LIKE TO **KNOW**, THAT'S ALL.

DARLING, THE PARKERS FROM Nº3 ARE DOING SOME RESEARCH INTO S.E.X.

THAT'S RIGHT JUST A FEW QUESTIONS. YOU KNOW WHAT YOU GET UP TO! YOUR LITTLE WAYS. YOUR HABITS!

YOUR **PRIVATE** HABITS!

OH! WELL I DON'T THINK WE HAVE ANY OF THOSE. HAVE WE?

I DON'T THINK SO DEAR.

YOU **HAVEN'T?** WELL IN THAT CASE...

YOU APPEAR TO HAVE BEEN WASTING OUR TIME!

GREAT SCRABBLE CONTEST

ZYXOMMA! WHAT ABOUT ZYXOMMA?

COME ON! CAN I HAVE ZYXOMMA? LET'S HAVE A RULING! CAN I HAVE IT? IS ZYXOMMA OKAY?

WELL, YES I THINK SO...

IT **IS?** FANTASTIC!

WHEN I GET THOSE LETTERS I WILL BEAR THAT IN MIND!